THE DEAD ALIVE AND BUSY

PHOENIX POETS

A SERIES EDITED BY ALAN SHAPIRO

the
dead
alive
and
busy

ALAN SHAPIRO

THE UNIVERSITY OF CHICAGO PRESS
Chicago and London

ALAN SHAPIRO is professor of English and creative writing at
the University of North Carolina, Chapel Hill. He is the
author of six books of poetry, most recently of *Mixed
Company,* which won the 1996 *Los Angeles Times* prize for
poetry. His memoir, *The Last Happy Occasion,* was a finalist
for the 1996 National Book Critics Circle award for biogra-
phy/autobiography. His most recent memoir, *Vigil,* appeared
in 1997. Shapiro was the winner of the 1999 O. B. Hardison,
Jr. Poetry Prize from the Folger Shakespeare Library.

The University of Chicago Press, Chicago 60637
The University of Chicago Press, Ltd., London
© 2000 by The University of Chicago
All rights reserved. Published 2000
Printed in the United States of America

09 08 07 06 05 04 03 02 01 00   1 2 3 4 5

ISBN: 0-226-75050-7 (cloth)
ISBN: 0-226-75051-5 (paper)

Library of Congress Cataloging-in-Publication Data

Shapiro, Alan, 1952–
        The dead alive and busy / Alan Shapiro.
            p.   cm.
        ISBN 0-226-75051-5 (pbk. : alk. paper). —
        ISBN 0-226-75050-7 (cloth : alk. paper)
        I. Title.
        PS3569.H338D43   2000   99-28802
        811'.54—DC21   CIP

for Della, first and last, now and always

The track of fled souls, and their Milkie-way.
The dead alive and busie . . .
—HENRY VAUGHAN

Contents

Acknowledgments

A note of gratitude is owing to the editors of the journals and books below, in which versions of these poems have appeared.

Alaska Quarterly: "Invisible Termini" (as "Another Day")
Agni Review: "Calypso, Penelope"
Boulevard: "The Summoning"
Meridian: "The Bath," "The Sanctuary," "The Dawn Walkers"
The New Yorker: "The Singer"
Paris Review: "Dream of the Dead"
Ploughshares: "The Coat," "What"
Poetry: "Bedtime Story, 1979"
River Styx: "Air," "Rose," "Scree," "The Table"
Slate: "Hallway," "Old Joke," "The Naked Eye" (www.slate.com.
      Copyright©1998 Microsoft Corporation. Reprinted by permission.)
Threepenny Review: "Feet," "Hermes," "Abraham and Isaac"
TriQuarterly: "Interstate," "New Year's Eve in the Aloha Room"

"On Men Weeping" was published in *A Store of Joys: Writers Celebrate the
      North Carolina Museum of Art's Fiftieth Anniversary* (Winston-
      Salem: Blair, 1997) Copyright©1997 by North Carolina Museum
      of Art Foundation. Reprinted by permission of North Carolina
      Museum of Art.

"Scree," "Hand," "Air," "Rose," "The Table," and "The Summoning"
      appeared in *Vigil* (Chicago: University of Chicago Press, 1997).

"The Coat" was selected for inclusion in the anthology *Best American Poetry 1998,* edited by John Hollander (New York: Scribner).

"Old Joke" was selected for inclusion in the anthology *The Handbook of Heartbreak,* edited by Robert Pinsky (New York: Morrow, 1999).

"Feet," "Thrush in Summer," "The Beach Chair," and "The Singer" appeared in *Contemporary American Poetry: Bread Loaf Anthology* (University Press of New England, 1999).

"The Bath" appeared in *Jewish American Poetry: A Collection of Essays,* edited by Jonathan Barron and Eric Murphy Selinger (University Press of New England, 1999).

The Dead Alive and Busy was greatly enabled by a fellowship term at the Institute for the Arts and Humanities at the University of North Carolina, Chapel Hill. This book was supported by a grant from the Project on Death in America of the Open Society Institute.

Old Joke

Radiant child of Leto, farworking Lord Apollo,
with lyre in hand and golden plectrum, you sang to the gods
on Mount Olympus almost as soon as you were born.

You sang, and the Muses sang in answer, and together
your voices so delighted all your deathless elders
that their perfect happiness was made more perfect still.

What was it, though, that overwhelmed them, that suffused,
astonished, even the endless ether? Was it the freshest,
most wonderful stops of breath, the flawless intervals

and scales whose harmonies were mimicking in sound
the beauty of the gods themselves, or what you joined
to that, what you were singing of, our balked desires,

the miseries we suffer at your indifferent hands,
devastation and bereavement, old age and death?
Farworking, radiant child, what do you know about us?

Here is my father, half blind, and palsied, at the toilet,
he's shouting at his penis, Piss, you! Piss! Piss!
but the penis (like the heavenly host to mortal prayers)

is deaf and dumb; here, too, my mother with her bad knee,
on the eve of surgery, hobbling by the bathroom,
pausing, saying, who are you talking to in there?

and he replies, no one you would know, sweetheart.
Supernal one, in your untested mastery,
your easy excellence, with nothing to overcome,

and needing nothing but the most calamitous
and abject stories to prove how powerful you are,
how truly free, watch them as they laugh so briefly,

godlike, better than gods, if only for a moment
in which what goes wrong is converted to a rightness,
if only because now she's hobbling back to bed

where she won't sleep, if only because he pees at last,
missing the bowl, and has to get down on his knees
to wipe it up. You don't know anything about us.

On Men Weeping

1. MVP

He was The Man, he said—"Understand what I'm saying"—
out there tonight, The Man. So while his teammates capered,
hollered and whooped in victory's unembarrassable light,
he having done at last what he set out to do, his whole life
flexed for so long in the expectation he would do it,
having met the rigors of the challenge, the challenge's exactions
and observances, met and surpassed them each one in turn,
The Man, the superstar, was weeping as he raised the trophy,
weeping as he caressed it, kissed it, the taut face so finely chiseled
to a single purpose now a dishevelment of tears, the body's muscled
concentration gone, the body all limp with the release of it.

Weeping the way he wept, it seemed, was what he won for,
as if the trophy in his arms, in his swoon of touching, were
the glistening proof he'd now gone far enough into his manhood
to be able to go freely back in time before it, as if the prize
for having proved he was The Man was that he got to be the boy,
the baby, weeping the way Achilles must have wept
because he could weep now, the bronze gear recovered,
the degraded foe behind him dragged in a wake of dust,
the war car circling the dead friend's opulent pyre, foremost
among the grieving warriors, like a boy, a slave girl, weeping,
bloody, behind the massive shield that only he could lift.

2. The Family Face

My father had no prerogative of tears, not in the stark arena
of the rest of us, not after he had filed out with his sisters
from the back parlor sealed off like a privy where
the body of his father lay. Only there behind the door
the stone-faced courteous usher closed, stood guard before,
in the dim light that would have kept his face apologetically
half hidden even from his sisters circling the casket,
only there was he allowed to give in at last and wail
the way he hadn't since he was a child. Yes, only there.

For when they filed out past us toward the waiting cars,
only he could not stop crying, having given himself too
freely over to his keening to realize where he was now,
that he was back among us, so that his brother-in-law,
his sister's husband, Joe, the millionaire, the lord and
magistrate of what the family exacted, was obliged to say
in front of all of us, so all of us could hear, "Hey Harold,
cut it out, you're gonna set the girls off all over again."
And he did, immediately he cut it out, abashed, his hands

a moment covering his face, he choked back what he had
no right to, what he hadn't earned. For who was he after all?
What was he worth, the second son, the clerk, the diligent
but ever struggling provider, with a wife who worked?
No way to lift the shield, no way to prove he could except
to recompose his face as a man's face, Joe's face, brittle,
cleansed of feeling—while Joe two decades later, even months
beyond her funeral, in front of everyone would sob for his wife
with all the inconsolable abandon that he had put away.

New Year's Eve in the Aloha Room

for Robert Cantwell, adapting a phrase of his
—Sherman Oaks, California, 1996

The dance floor is an oval incandescence
against the dark, and they are spectral in it,
my mother and father, as they glide across.
It's taken them half a century to get here.
Although his hand shakes, and her back is stooped,
he's in his pinstripes, she in her green taffeta.
Nearly midnight. The calendar pages flutter
backward in the breeze of melody,
her eyes half closed, *embrace me*, she is smiling,
moving as if alone, the way a girl does
before a mirror, twirling and swaying in
and out of an imagined lover's arms,
while he looks on, *don't be a naughty baby*,
his face lordly with pleasure, pleasure of mastery—
come to papa, come to papa, do—
that's so complete it's more anticipation
than control, the way his hand, *my sweet*
embraceable you, his fingers hardly need
to touch her fingers, guiding her every move.
The pages flutter backward in the breeze.
It's taken them half a century to get here.

Beyond the dance floor, in the shadows there
are stockyards at the outskirts of the city;
there are mills and foundries, and along the Charles,
the abattoir has shut down for the night:
there is no work tomorrow, and they can be
only their best ideas about themselves,
their bodies, embraceable, aristocratic,
they are peasants with a little cash to burn,
don't be a naughty baby, they are greenhorns,
come to papa, in the New World dreaming
not of a levelling of rich and poor—
the Irish are all lushes, the Negroes lazy—
but a carnival reversal, *come to papa*
come to papa do. It's nearly midnight,
nearly a new millennium. There have been wars.
There have been foreclosures and estrangements,
a son's divorce, a daughter's death. But now,
the pages fluttering backward as they dance,
it's all forgotten, even unforeseen.
How young they are, and hopeful. Let's leave them now
before the song ends, and they wake, bewildered,
in the Aloha Room, to everything
it's taken them half a century to get.

Vase of Flowers

More difficult to bear, more difficult
somehow to look at than the body on the bed,
the body of her daughter, is the vase
of flowers on the bedside table. Absurd
machinery of metamorphosis,
the way they go on breathing, sucking water
up through the cut stems, cell by cell, into
the petalled radiance the water feeds
and, as it feeds them, lifts away as scent
beyond the petals, diffusing, fanning out
into the air as seamlessly as air
fans from the open window into sky.
Someone should stop it. Someone should switch it off
as faraway as the pale gauze of sunrise,
as near as where the dawn light hasn't reached,
magnolia blossoms ghostly in a cave
of leaves beyond the window, and below them,
among the shadows where someone is walking,
someone unseeable if not for the white
fluorescence of the uniform that seems
to float free of the body, back and forth

across the blacktop of the drive—absurd
machinery of water into whiteness,
of whiteness into scent, out of the vase,
over the underworld her daughter is,
inside the room and out of it, up and down,
from sky to earth, from earth to Acheron.

Feet

Feet he can't lift, feet padding with a toddler's half-
step, sh-sh-sh, down the carpeted hall, feet swollen,
purple, with minuscule white cracks between the toes,
along the sides, the heel, sore feet he's asking me,
if it's, you know, no bother, will I rub with cream?

dry feet I gingerly cup and lift into my lap,
feet of the stockyard, feet of the slaughterhouse, factory,
showroom floor, my fingers working the moisturizer
down into the parched soles, the rinds of calluses,
over the bunched skin rough as braille above the heel bone,

the instep whitening under the pressure of my touch,
then darkening again, whitening then darkening,
lifted and let down, feet of the love bed, feet of we had
a few good years before the war, before you children,
feet of I never cheated on her, I never beat her,

what the hell else does she want? First one and then the other,
cupped in my hand, cupped even as I let them down
so slowly that the weight, the gravity, the pulling
from the earth's core for a moment's mine, not theirs, then theirs
again, half-stepping sh-sh-sh down the carpeted hall.

Aphrodite

The gold adorned, the lover of smiles, is nearing.
Even the animal skins upon the bed,
the many skins of bear and lion that
Anchises, like in beauty to the gods,
has slaughtered, skinned with his own hands, even they
can sense her moving nearer down the steep
slope of Mt. Ida's woods, the draws and meadows,
among the secret springs; can feel already
in the soft fur she'll lie against with him
a quickening memory of what they were.

Anchises, too, feels something, he doesn't know what.
The sudden restlessness that makes him wander
outside the hut, with lyre in hand, is how
she's coming to him now, her every step
another note between the fingertip
and string, between the string and voice that sings
vague dream sounds trembling nearly into song,
like reveries of reveries, of conquest,
indefinite renown that as she nears
are necklaces, gold brooches, earrings his hand
will unclasp gently, raiments that his hand
will loosen and let fall away from whom
he'll lead by hand into the readied bed,
between the coverings of bear and lion.

The gold adorned is coming, the lover of smiles.
All over Ida all the predators
are stirred to follow: those that are sleeping wake
now as she passes; they come out of the inner
passages of caves, they rise from shadowy lairs,
from dens and coverts. Even the ravenous ones,
gray wolves and bears, lions and quick leopards,
ravenous for deer, in mid-stride, ready
to strike, their jaws already opening,
are suddenly halted, turned as in a dream
in the direction of her sharpening scent.

The Bath

When he called me to help him from the tub that he had somehow,
despite his blindness, palsied hands, bad back and shoulder,

gotten himself into without falling, so in the water's heat,
his body nearly forgotten, he could rest and doze,

but now lay shivering in, naked before me, helpless,
the penis slack and floating beneath the belly fat,

the spindleshanks, loose swags of flesh along the arms,
we needed customary speech but knew no custom.

This was a desolate place. Forget Ham and his father's, "Cursed
be Canaan, a slave of slaves shall he be to his brothers."

There was no curse or blessing here. If there were guides,
or avatars among us, speaking the words for us

to speak, of broken covenants, of dereliction,
and redress, we heard them only as the faint,

miasmal whispering of our embarrassment.
Forget Aeneas and Anchises. There was no place

for us to go to after I turned my back, and knelt,
and with his arm around my neck, lifted him slowly

piggyback from the water, his head against mine,
our faces there in the mirror facing us, side by side,

with nothing to say except he's okay, I can leave now,
god damn it he can dry himself, and so I let him.

Worm

Why isn't she happier? Why isn't it
enough for her her son has found, at last,
some honor in the world? Of course she's proud.
What mother wouldn't be? She's not a monster.
It's only that the long dreamed of reward
for all her waiting and preparing seems
too late, if not too little, since her sisters,
the only ones she wants to share the good
news with, are dead. Who's left for her to call?
What should be honey in her mouth is ashes
because she can't tell them, because the more
she says to no one, Anne, look what he's done,
the more she says to no one, Look, Irene,
look what my son has done, the more she feels
it was to spite her that they died, died only
to turn the honey in her mouth to ashes
no different from the ashes that the years
of longing for that honey were before.
Ashes to ashes. What did she expect?
Always the good sister, happy enough
for their sake even while her son was taking
his own sweet time to prove himself, shiftless
for so long, stubbornly unambitious, she
was happy enough to listen for hours on end
to their my son the this, my daughter that.

So now when it's her turn to call, is it
too much to ask that they return the favor,
let her for once, this one time, lord her glory
over them, as she let them? What,
she can't help feeling, is the payoff but
the lousy exchange of one dream for another?
Isn't their final triumph now that she
should have to dream of going back in time,
all the way back to childhood where her sisters,
amazed, admiring, seeing her as she is now,
read in the radiant visage of her joy
the name that shall remain that shall be her
name, hers and her descendants, who shall go forth
and look upon the bodies of the dead
whose names shall not be known, for whom alone
the worm that eats them shall not die, for whom
the fire alone that burns them shall never be quenched?

The Sanctuary

Somewhere in a book about the camps,
caught in articulate sentences, among
precise descriptions of the causal chains
of small coincidences, the step by step
emergence of the will, the protocols,
the rational mechanisms, is a man
who every morning, till his final morning,
despite how weak he may have been, or sick,
even in winter, in the freezing air,
surrounded by all the other nameless ones,
would strip his clothes off, bend over a sink
that wasn't there and with imagined water
flowing from an imaginary tap
fastidiously scrub his face, his neck,
armpits and genitals.

                    Here in the room
in which I write these words, one moment it's
the nameless man I see, the next my father,
his palsied hand lifting the fork so shakily
that by the time it finally gets from plate
to mouth the food is mostly gone, and he
is mostly eating air for dinner, though
he keeps on eating till his plate is clean.

Inside the room in which I write this down,
somewhere inside a chapter of the book
I haven't taken from the shelf in years,
on that page, and on this one, his and my father's
bodies in the motion of a dream
of normalcy are held, preserved, protected
within a kind of sanctuary where,
bad as it surely is, it can't get worse.

Over and over, one chews his phantom food,
the other washes with imagined water.
Only subservient to the rules of grammar,
inside the rational structure of the lines,
in soundless sentences and scentless words,
one lifts the dish towel like a serviette,
dabs delicately at his mouth, his chin,
before he gets up shakily and all
the food falls from his lap onto the floor;
the other now meticulously puts
the foul rags on again, as if they were
a suit or uniform, and he were someone
on any normal day with work to do.

Hallway

Too uncomfortable to sleep,
and too tired not to, wandering
in a half-sleep all night
through the small apartment,
the good leg dragging the bad
behind it like a child
to punishment, the back
stooped, and the head cocked
slightly like a bird's so he can see
with the eye that isn't blind yet
just where the hell he's going—

if he isn't one of Plato's
souls that walk out to the rim
of heaven, consider him,
at least, the fleshed-out
idea, the bodily perfection
of everything they would
have had to overcome
to get there; consider him
the why me, arthritic subtext
of their aspiration, what it is,
as they gaze upon the fixed,

impersonal shining of
the good, the just, the beautiful,
that wanders through the small
apartment all night long
from bedroom to hall, from hall
to kitchen, kitchen to bathroom,
the whole time thinking
only of sleep, and how
much longer can he walk
like this, and what will he do
with himself, at night, when he can't.

Hermes

In the old story no sooner are the suitors
slaughtered than they go flittering like bats
behind you, shrilling their ineffectual cries.
My father, though, you piecemeal lead away,
marshall of dreams, tireless errand boy,
flashing before him in the shape of dead
friends and relations at every intersection,
on the way to and from the hospital,
or pharmacy, whenever we're stopped in traffic,
at a long light, he listing over, his head
against my shoulder, dozing sometimes and sometimes
mumbling snatches of whatever song
is on the radio. Then you appear,
dissembler, among the people crossing before us,
flashing and disappearing among the buzzcuts
and dreadlocks, shopping carts and boom boxes.
Whenever he says, "Lester, that's Lester Cohen,
what the hell's he doing here?" or "Hey! there's Max,
Max Lambke," or "Isn't that my brother Amos?"—
before he laughs, shaking his head and slips
back into sleep or song, it's you he sees,
your entourage, winding its slow way past us,

taking him piecemeal with you from the corner
of Fairfax and San Vincente, of Beverly Glen
and Sunset, down the mouldering paths beyond
the Ocean's streams, beyond the White Rock and
the Western Gates, and past the Land of Dreams
into the smoky fields of asphodel.

Departure

What is devotion?

                        He had come outside
to watch me go. The cab was waiting,
I had a plane to catch, a family, a job
to return to.
                Tell me about dignity—

                                    He was just

standing there in his boxers
and t-shirt, on the bright green
carpet of fake grass, between
the stone deer and the bronze egret,
among the stunted palm trees.
                          And love?

                                   Behind him

I could hear the harrowingly
bland voice of the play-by-play
announcer saying it was fourth and goal,
    "There's still plenty of time remaining."
    The crowd was going crazy.
                        What good

did love do either of you then?
                        I waved

before I got into the cab
but he just stood there staring,
as the blind do, vaguely in my direction.

"Awesome baby—all the hard work,
   the sacrifice, the long days and nights—
   it all comes down to this."
One hand was balled up in a fist
to keep from trembling.

The Dawn Walkers

Down the flat beach they come, the dawn walkers,
in the still cool air, along the slow continuous
roaring of the breakers, and phantasmal foam

they could be conjured from, on bad or soon-
to-be-bad knees, on joints no warming up
can take the stiffness out of now; the hale,

the not so hale, the tentative shufflers
and baby-steppers, two by two, or singly,
walk over the sand that giving way beneath them

tilts them forward, as if uphill they go,
pushing themselves, both Sisyphus and stone,
both stone and hill, pushing a heavy stone

that every step makes heavier up a hill
that's growing ever steeper as they push.
How far do we have to go? their bodies ask.

In every bead of sweat that stings their eyes,
each quickened pant, their bodies feel the night
press down against them through the brightened sky.

They feel it, and they falter, and they ask,
how far? how far? And then they right themselves
and push on, answering, not now, not yet.

II

After the Hurricane

Can you lift up your voice to the clouds,
that a flood of waters may cover you?
Can you send forth lightnings, that they may go
and say to you, "Here we are?"
                        —from the Book of Job

The neighborhood was gone. Where patios had been,
yards, fences, gardens, driveway and street, was now a flood
of downed trees our houses seemed to float in, half submerged.

We clambered out over the tangled sprawl of limbs,
root systems dangling in the air above the black
pits they were ripped from, power lines twisted, vine-like,

around the vines that twisted around the every-which-
way scattered trunks, and here and there far from their corners
were stop signs and street names under us, adrift in branches,

their metal crumpled like tissue. Your ways are not our ways.
As if the slow work of our hands, what we had cleared,
bounded and built up block by block were nothing but

a gossamer vexation you could sweep away
whenever you wanted to. O Voice out of the whirlwind,
we heard and were afraid, and fearing you, were made

transparent to each other, vividly unreal,
too close to the loud core of your questioning
not to hear it even after we backed away,

returned to our private damages, uncertain holdings—
even then we couldn't drown it out as all day long,
and in the days that followed, up and down the street,

our chainsaws in a storm of sawdust screamed and screamed,
our clenched, exhilarated hands jerking the teeth
down deeper, harder through the bark and sap and heartwood,

jerking them through the way a leash jerks when the dog
is bad, won't listen, doesn't come when we say come,
or heel when we say heel, or when we say stop stop.

Interstate

First it's late day, and no car stops or slows, or even
seems to see me here, thumb out, and shivering,
by the exit where hours ago my last ride let me off.

And then it's night, and no car anywhere at all,
only white highway, and a hissing snow, and now
and again a semi ramming past, its shrill horn blaring,

and in its wake the silence rushing back around me
denser each time, a little more unbreakable,
like death in dreams, death without loss of consciousness.

So when at last light flashes vaguely through the snow swirl,
and a car slows, pulling over up ahead, exhaust
all rosy in the taillights, the door already open,

the luck I earlier expected, wished for, prayed for,
abandoned any hope of, now seems otherworldly,
as if an angel's intervened, except the angel

reeks of Brut, his face ambiguous, wrinkled and
babyish beneath the yellow pageboy haircut,
a middle-age cherub, smiling in the scent-cloyed

warmth I lean through, thick flakes tumbling off my arms,
my shoulders, whirling in out of the night behind me
over the (are they?) brochures he's sweeping off the seat.

And for a moment as I pull the door shut, there is
cloudless sky under my boots, palm trees, bright water,
and bikinied women on a bone-white stretch of beach.

"Wish you were there, I bet. You have the body for it."
Boston, I tell him. I'm going to Boston. "Your lucky night,"
he says, not glancing at me, staring straight ahead.

And now it's only thinking of the night and snow
surrounding us, of being stranded there, that makes
it possible for me to feel the warmth as warmth,

the luck as good, that gets me through it all the way
to Boston, slow mile after mile, our minuet
of innuendo, he touching my arm, my shoulder,

whenever he asks about me, do I go to school? who
are my girlfriends? what do we do together? and I,
as I answer, leaning away, but not too far, just far

enough for him to think that maybe I haven't noticed,
I'm not afraid, just tired, he hasn't been rebuffed.
See how the two pans of the scale are trembling:

kindness and appetite, courtesies of deflection,
fear and deceit, as he follows my directions, pulls up
before the wrong apartment I have said is mine,

a block from where I live. See how the two pans tremble,
how precarious the balance, diffidence, restraint,
his asking shyly if maybe I want a drink,

my "sorry," his "of course not," embarrassment, relief,
snow freakish in the headlights as he pulls away,
the clean consoling chill of snow all over me,

my own bed warmer for it, warmer till he almost
seems an angel, having delivered me at last
to where it's all warm sand, bright water, and the woman

I imagine here beside me goes on touching me
as he, in his own bed, might now imagine me,
his angel, touching him in every way he wants,

his angel, mine, the two pans floating evenly,
without the slightest tremor, the kindness only kind,
the pleasure pleasure, the fingertips as soft as air.

The Naked Eye

The small stage he's sitting snug against is radiant
as an operating table on which the naked dancer
doubled in the mirrored backdrop dances before him
simultaneously from both sides at once, blond crotch
and jiggling ass, nipple and churning shoulder blade.

If he's aware of us at all, my friends and I,
in a back booth farthest from the stage, what are we
but the proverbial rubes, sightseeing frat boys
on a sleazy lark, too loud, too talkative, giggling
uneasy ironies about being where we'd never go alone.

If we annoy him, the annoyance must be somehow
necessary to his pleasure, the rising of it sweeter
for the last tug of a defeated gravity—as feeble
now, as faraway, as being anybody's son or father.
For he seems all gaze, nudging a dollar toward her.

And she, her back to him, seems only what she shows
as she bends over, reaching between her splayed legs
to pick it up, her face a moment upside down
beneath her crotch, her pink tongue flickering level
with the face she watches watching her, the face void

of expression, dense as stone, clinical as light,
unmoved, as if the fantasy is that there isn't one,
that she isn't dancing any gesture of what she
imagines he imagines she would feel like if he
were doing to her what she pretends he does.

The fantasy is wholly of the eye. The eye is his.
The eye is lordly. Only imagine it as thinking:
Let the frat boys hoard how her fingertips have eased
the hidden lips back to the moist interior, let them
smuggle home to other women pale simulations

of themselves still outside watching what they only
enter in the dark, what in the dark they only feel—
Only imagine it, and it is yours, your eye, and mine,
no less imperiously moving over him as his moves
over the places in her she has never seen.

It is a seer's eye moving lordly through the bar,
over all of us its rapture cool, so otherworldly,
who here can deny that hidden craving is abroad,
and that the cure lies in the body spread before us
that the eye alone is shrewd enough to read.

Furies

The invisible furies our local madman rants at
over his shoulder as they goad him along
unceasingly from corner to corner, up

and down each street, through every intersection,
wherever it's busiest, wherever there are people
to stand aside and gawk, have all eased up

today, grown mild, almost companionable:
the rage of nonsense they harry out of him
quelled to a whisper as he strolls among us,

smiling and nodding, unhurried, confident,
a celebrity among admirers,
a lord deigning to mingle, and yet mingling

with such effortless yet subtle courtesy
that no one notices how little he needs
the adulation he graciously accepts.

Wherever he goes, it seems, they're there behind him,
there at his ear, his whispering advisers,
factotums, handlers, look this way, sir, won't you?

Chemical hellhounds of a violation
inside his body going back, maybe,
to childhood, or even farther back, the debt

too old to be repaid, though every moment
they demand full payment, unappeasable,
even when they appear to be appeased,

their mildness another aspect of the torture,
as now he turns to see the face before him
in the plate glass windows, ghost-like, drifting through

and over lingerie and nightgowns, suits,
shoes, jewelry, and luggage, from store to store,
the things that anyone on any day

might buy, the face, too, nearly anyone's.
Whose is it? Why are you doing this to me?
the muscles all defused along the jaw,

the head not twitching, the long hair calm, the face
you recognize it, don't you, sir, milord,
Mr. President? of what he may have been,

or never was, the torment now much worse
for the serene reminder there beside him,
right there yet out of reach, out of reach

yet inescapable, dogging his every step.

Invisible Termini

Invisible termini, elusive and inevitable
thresholds of innumerable things I once
couldn't imagine never doing and now discover
I no longer do, discover I had done them
for the last time only when the last time is itself
beyond recalling on a day when something else
I did is being done, unknowingly, for good.

The way each night for years my mother bathed me,
each night her hands upon my body, her hands playful
and free upon my body in the lather sliding
over every part of me, calf, thigh and belly,
frontside and back, night after night our candid pleasure
never hinting of a last night, never saying
that what went on as if it always would would not.

Invisible termini, unnoticeable thresholds,
finalities approaching, even now, this morning,
the way my little daughter naked at the top of the stairs
likes how it feels as her hand between her plump thighs
burrows in, caresses, touches, so engrossed
in pleasure that she hardly hears me calling her
to get dressed already, Daddy has to get to work.

Sensation frank as breathing, boundless as air, her self
fast in the Eden of herself, the gate still far
enough away to let her go on doing what
she does in front of me, to let me watch her do it
and not even need to hide how much I want to,
how much I like it, though because I do I hide
it anyway and say, again, come on, it's late.

I climb the stairs. I realize as I swoop her up
into my arms how freely my hand roams, still can roam
all over her until we laugh again, as always,
as if we always will, as if no gate were opening
even now, no threshold nearing, no other day
lying in wait to catch us unaware within
its widening hesitations, narrowing delights.

What

After I flung you down
at last onto the bed
because it was two a.m.
and you'd been crying for hours,
it seemed, and would not stop,
all my comforting
defeated, spent; because
you were too frantic by then
to say what it was you wanted,
sobbing too much to say it,
though you kept on trying
to say it till you were frantic
now because I didn't
understand; in the stunned moment
after I flung you down,
before you wailed again,
in your amazed look

I saw how having done
to you just that much had
already brought me that
much closer to doing more;

I saw how memory
in me is a collapsing
universe sucked back
in toward its black
original adhesion,
while in you it is
a universe too suddenly
expanded where my never
before seen or suspected
fury whirls away
forever now as
what might happen
from what you won't recall.

Abraham and Isaac

1.

Think of the story as two dreams.
In the first, I am the boy
bound to the altar
which my father mounts,
his knees against my chest,
the knife raised. Far from our dwellings,
motherless, in the flexed
muscle of the scene,
as he leans down, I feel
less bewilderment, less
terror than relief,
as if I've never not
been here, though never here
so clearly:
the eyes brightened
to frank readiness,
the shut mouth, the fingers
whitening around the handle
now seem wholly possessed
by what before, in real time,
among the women,
would flare and die out
in balked hints,

unwilled gestures, looks
that could only sharpen
the vigilance
they momentarily escaped.

I realize that he never
until now so much as
raised his hand against me
not because he wasn't angry,
but because he always was,
the very urge fed
by the decision to forbid it,
keener to us both
with each caress, more fearful
the less recognized it was,
so that it seems,
under the cover of what the Father
of all fathers has commanded,
that we both feel
something entirely our own
yet older than ourselves,
as if some alien weight
had suddenly been lifted,
the lightness of it so
exhilarating that
what horrifies us
is our disappointment
when the ram appears.

2.

But in the second dream
when it's you bound to the altar,
your face where mine was,

mine where his,
the only way to prove
I'm not my father, being yours,
and being my son, you aren't me,
is not to hear the ram
thrash in the thicket,
not to let the angel's hand
keep my hand poised
forever in a begotten
and begetting fury, but
at last to bring it down
against you and behold
in the bewilderment and terror
of your every feature just
how inconceivable it is
that I would ever do
to you what I am doing.

The Coat

Not night now, not the night's
one chilling vocable
of sharp air, not the cross
parental babble of it
burning your infant ear,
not anything you say
in answer, no good, not fair,
the fiercest syllables
that turn, as soon as spoken,
into steam that lifts away,

no, none of these is the
beloved in the story.
There's no beloved, none,
except the coat you wear,
the heavy coat you've clung
so long, so hard to that
the only warmth you sense
now is the warmth that seeks
an arctic bitterness
to hoard itself against.

Here you are easiest
where only phantom shapes
across the honeyed vagueness
of the window pass—
easiest where no lock
is turned, no door is opened,
no one at all to find
in your greeting that the coat
that kept you warm outside
has brought the cold in with it.

Bedtime Story, 1979

We who agree
        on nothing are
                agreed on this

too vigilant
        and thorough
                disenchantedness.

Here, at least,
        if nowhere else, is
                common ground,

fixed vantage
        of a shared estrangement
                where we find,

it seems, the truth
        of who we
                really are together:

our intimacy more
        tense border crossing
                than a pleasure,

and pleasure less
        a grace accepted,
                grace bestowed,

than a precise,
        sly adding up
                of all we're owed.

The love we thought
        immune to all
                vicissitude,

as free, as
        inexhaustible
                as the charmed food

in a child's
        story, food
                replenishing itself

as it's consumed,
        desire filled
                as soon as felt,

as soon as filled
        renewed, as if
                our unabated

hunger for
        each other was
                itself what sated—

that love is now
        more like the story
                when, at last,

the child who resisted
        sleep for pleasure
                is sleeping fast,

the quaint book put
        back on the shelf
                where it is kept,

the shade pulled shut,
        the light extinguished,
                the room left.

Calypso, Penelope

Fixed noon of her white
robe's watery
shimmer as it slid down
from her shoulders, all
the way down around her
till the very air,
as she moved toward him,
evening after evening,
all those years there
with her on her island,
was suffused with having
once again that first
glance, first touch,
of her frank inviting.

It was as if he lived
in the perpetual
arrival of that single
moment, in a having
that the salt skurl
of no having had
could follow, no want
precede, both somehow
at the same time weaving
constantly their now

illusory shadows
over her to turn
her perfect brightness
even brighter still;

his pleasure in her made
more fresh and sudden
for the restless weaving
of those phantom thirsts,
hungers, obsolescent
incompletenesses
her ever changing
changeless beauty
simultaneously
aroused and filled.
Spellbound in the breathless
home of her unstinted
giving he was no one
he had ever been.

He was too visible.
No place inside him
unpossessed enough
even to ponder, call
back and play over
all in his own way
the sheer art (or was it
utter artlessness?)
of what they did together.
That's why he wanted
to go home, home
to his old bed, to
memory born
in an expiring pleasure,

time's intricate privacies,
the never not receding,
dense, too numerous
horizons he's continually
at one and the same time
setting out toward
and returning from—
as if to be at home there
were forever to be
voyaging in secret
over other kinds
of seas, in chancier
weather, laden with need,
with curiosity,

the opaque intimacy
of the half-fulfilled,
half-said, half-given,
where his wife, the ever
circumspect, will want
to ask him only this
much and no more
as they lie back
in the ritual aftermath
of passion: What, what
are you thinking of? and he,
the ever resourceful,
can tell her nothing, nothing,
as he draws her close.

The Singer

The way you sang, half-dozing as I drove,
the radio on; the way your hovering
so near sleep, unaware of me, appeared
to purify your shyness, not free you from it;
the way you needed even then to sing
without appearing to, your hushed voice lagging
with a furtive clumsiness behind the singer's,
each syllable only half-formed on your lips
before the next one and the next arrived;
the way you happily seemed to falter after
what was always half a syllable beyond—
was not the least accomplished of your many
unknowingly disclosed when most disguised
most accidental flashings of a presence
that's not for yours but other people's eyes.

Thrush in Summer

Aged as Hardy's thrush, frail, gaunt, but silent,
not flitting away, or even flinching there
in the azalea when I pull back branches
and lean in, my face just inches from you now.
The eye you eye me with is a drop of tar,
glassy and blank; the bent twig of your beak
is shut; your gray-brown plumage ragged, blast-
beruffled, though the day is calm, though there
is only a calm morning's drift of pale
and dark green shadows rippling the air,
with every moment now a different sound
of bird song high up in the trees, throughout
the understory, everywhere around us,
it seems, the day is singing in its shapes
and sounds and colors the full-hearted song
you sang once in another century,
another season, while beyond the poem,
mutely, your body sings the song you sang
against, of frost and wind, the shrunken pulse,
the weakening eye of day that this new day
is singing over, blessedly unaware.

The Beach Chair

for David Ferry

The leaves drift in a clatter and dry hiss
over the beach chair left out in the yard
since summer: its symmetries and surfaces,
the taut green fabric of its back and seat,
the dull sheen of its frame, are aswarm with leaves
that fall all afternoon into the shadows
of leaves that haven't fallen yet and now
seem almost to be rising from within
the form they float on up to what's falling down.
It is as if by holding still, it holds
each instant's omen and its memory,
omens of altering, and memories
of having altered, as the leaves, brittle
as coral, reticulating through the air
in swirls and drifts, fall toward the shadowy sway
of leaves about to fall along the planes
and angles of what happens to be there.

Ghost

Ghost of the living body
given shape and texture
by what the body is
denied, spectrum of desire
colorful when impeded,
white when not—since
at the end your love for me
was mostly fantasy,
and since fantasy became
a way of keeping faith,
of being present, let
it be your fantasy
tonight that I am here
beside you speaking, that
these words are mine.

Here you are just as you were
a year ago, remember?
on your birthday, you
in the dark den, in your lap
a shot glass full of what
around that time you took
to calling your vitamin h,
your vitamin happy, the tv
on, the sound off, the screen

crosshatched with rubbery
bands of color that
would spasm into tit
or ass a moment then
be gone, so that you couldn't
tell if what you saw
was seen or just imagined.
How long had it been
since you had touched me?

I was too sick to care
by then, or to think much
about what it was like
between us before the cancer,
those times we couldn't get
enough of one another,
and how we afterward
would lie there side by side,
my back to you, you with
an arm curled under me,
the other over, your hands
moving (unable not
to) up and down from rib
to nipple, nipple to rib,
as if you thought my body
were your undeserved
good luck. But that was then.

Now I was bald, I had
one breast, it was your birthday,
and I'd forgotten, hadn't
bought you anything,
not even a cake, and when
I woke and found you there

in the dark, the tv flashing
like bad nerves in the shot
glass you were lifting slowly
to your lips, I suddenly
really for the first
time knew how hard it must
have been for you to look
at me and not flinch, not wish
the doctor had taken both
of my breasts, instead of leaving
one behind, one freakish
remnant of a normal woman.

I got on my knees, I kneeled
before you, but before
I could ask you to forgive me,
what could I do to make
it up to you? you took
my head in both hands, tilted
it sideways, gently, saying,
go down on me, honey,
come on, it's been so long,
make me happy, you
can do that for me, can't you?

You should have known
that I was done with that
by then, too far inside
my body's misery
for sex, for you, for
anything beyond
my wanting not to suffer.
But now it's gone, the body,
the misery's gone too,

like a jammed channel
that's suddenly unjammed,
the picture unobstructed,
so I can see how generous
you feel, as I go down on you,
how blind but generous,
the way one hand is resting
on my face, my cheek,
to guide it, coax it while
the other hand is reaching
through my nightgown's
collar, to cup the one
breast tenderly, gratefully,
as if another swayed
beside it, and as I make
you happy, as your eyes
close, and you say my name,
say it softly, sadly,
as if it were another
woman's name, as if
I were the woman you
were cheating on me with,
I can see at last just
what it is you think
you're doing: it's your birthday,
and in two months I'll be dead.
This is the last time I will
touch you in this way.
It is your birthday, you
are celebrating, you
are happy, handsome, and
your wife is beautiful.

Dream of the Dead

Not the tired figures of our own fatigue,
our misplaced envy, sleep eternal, peace
in the blank heaven of complete belonging.

Not steam on the hot pavement after rain,
the garbled rumors of a shape, a gesture
shy of the light, their gauzy shiftingness

itself too much confinement as each blurred
strand twists back in an agony of yearning
toward the dispersal they had risen from.

No, when the dead rose up before me, they,
the most recent dead as dead as the most ancient,
were the soul of fire without anything to burn,

hunger shorn of mouth, except the mouth,
the tinder, that our flesh provided, yours
and mine, for you and I were there, our naked

bodies now their entrance to a loved
estrangement, and as we began to move
together unaware, as the moistened skin

tensed slowly toward the sudden spasm, on
our vagrant lips, our curious fingers, over
every inch of us they burned and fed.

III

Scree

Long scree of pill bottles
        spilling over the tipped brim
of the wicker basket, fifty or more,
        a hundred,

your name on every one and under
        your name the brusque rune of instructions—
which ones to take, how many, and often,
        on what days,

with or without food, before or
        after eating, impossible
toward the end to keep them all straight,
        not even

with your charts, your calendars, the bottles
        ranged in sequence along the kitchen
counter—you always so
        efficient,

organized, never without a plan,
        even when planning had come down
to this and nothing more, for there was
        still a future

in it, though the future reached
        only from one bottle to
the next, from pill to pill, each one
        another

toehold giving way
        beneath you on the steep slope
you never stopped struggling against,
        unable not

to climb, and then, when climbing
        was impossible, not to try slowing
the quickening descent. You had
        descended now,

your body thinned to the machine
        of holding on, while I exhausted
by the vigil, with all your medicine
        spread before me,

looked for something, anything
        at all to help me sleep. To help me
for a short while anyway
        not be

aware of you, your gaunt hand
        clutching the guardrail, your eyes
blind, flitting, scanning, it seemed,
        the air above them

for their own sight, and the whimper
        far back in the throat, the barely
audible continuous
        half-cry half-

wheeze I couldn't hear and not think
        you were saying something, though
I couldn't make out what. I wanted
        to sleep,

I wanted if just for that one night
        to meet you there on that steep slope,
the two of us together, facing
        opposite

directions, I, because I wasn't
        dying, looking down, desiring
what you, still looking up, resisted,
        because you were.

Hand

You all but paralyzed, leashed to the catheter
that almost decorously slipped out from beneath the blanket,
running down under the guardrails to the urine bag

that no longer filled, since you'd stopped eating, drinking,
the body nearly now past feeding on itself,
past even that much agency—yet days before,

you were still able to get yourself up out of bed.
Dizzy with morphine that by then could only dull
the pain, not kill it, with your arm around my shoulder,

no matter how it hurt, you were determined to walk,
because you still could, to the bathroom, to complete
the marathon of five feet maybe, maybe six,

and on your own relieve yourself, and clean yourself,
and on your own stand up, and hug the nightgown to you
so it wouldn't slip from your shoulders, your privacy preserved,

protected, clung to, till you were safely back in bed.
Each stage of your decline, if it was hell
while you were in it, did it become too brief a heaven

once it had passed, as walking first, then privacy,
had passed, as these, too, would pass, these final vestiges
of will, of purpose, relief, if not exactly pleasure,

in the hand you, all but paralyzed, could barely lift,
but lifted, trembling, only inches from the bed
where it could flex, unflex, the fingers slowly closing

halfway toward the bony hollow of the palm,
closing and opening each time a little farther,
easier, until the numbness in the joints began

to loosen and retreat, and the hand could feel again
still capable of soothing itself, of being soothed,
before it fell at last like deadweight back to the bed?

Air

The Mexican woman in the room across from Beth's;
the teenage boy down the hall, the young man in the corner
room so shrivelled beneath the covers that the bed
looked always just made, smooth as if no one was in it;

the man in the next room who for days had been delirious,
violent, and after trying to choke his wife
whom he didn't recognize, had to be strapped down
until the tumor in his brain became restraint enough;

the black man with lung cancer who could have been
my age or my father's, and who, when he still could,
with his walker first, and then with his wheelchair, day
and night patroled the halls wheezing as he asked each

person, anybody, even the nurses, for a smoke,
a puff, come on, man, who's gonna know the difference;
and Beth herself, of course, all of the dying, each one,
in turn, when the end was near, would look away from us,

their faces drawn toward the window, toward the light outside,
more flower now than human, but still human, yearning
not for people, though—they seemed all done with that—
and not for grace, or mercy, or for any otherworldly

health, but only this, the air outside, the opalescent
flux of shade and sun dazzle there on the skin
as the body moves again and breathes in what is
always opening out around it wherever it goes.

Rose

The pump lay under the pillow where no one could see it.
Those nights when the morphine it released was not enough
to let her sleep, and Beth moaned weakly, thrashing a little,
turning her head from side to side, the pump would slip
out from beneath the pillow, dangling from her shoulder
where the thread-thin tube went in. Before I'd call the nurse,
I'd hold it in my hand. Its case, the size and shape
of the tv's remote control. I'd run my finger down
across the flat red button, trembling just to graze it,
cool as metal to the touch, yet so secure,
so tight within its socket that I could press on it lightly,
and then less lightly, and still it wouldn't budge. Ooh,
Beth would mutter over and over through pursed lips,
Ooh, her tremulous weak syllable of no ease,
ooh, and please, and if I pumped all of it out
into the suffering engine of her, so she at last
could sleep, so I too could sleep, who'd know? Who'd blame me?
Rose-red, the button was, flat bloom of coolest fire,
in the half-dark. When the nurse arrived to "boost" her,
that's what she'd call it, I'd leave the room, I'd walk the halls
to calm myself, to quell the shame of what I wanted
to do, the shame of being too afraid to do it—

and here and there I'd pass a room someone had died in
earlier that day. The door that had been kept shut
up to then, as ours was shut (was it to guard
our sorrow, by hiding it to think it ours alone,
peculiar to ourselves?), the door stood open now
because it opened on to no one, nothing, gone
the bouquets on the shelves, the pitiful toiletries,
cards on the feeding tray, pictures of children, all
the unbearable weight of each particular dying gone,
effaced, a gauze of sorrow swept thoroughly away,
and what remained was just the bed's amnesia,
immaculate white counterpane, white sheet, white rounded pillow,
and like a still opening red rupture on the void
it seemed to brighten from, absurdly beautiful,
where only hours before the head had lain, a rose.

Revenant

To have heard you, to have felt you with me, in me,
not in a dream, or if in dream, to know
dream as a porousness your being fills,

you as you are now, sentient vapor trail
of soul, and not some wished-for simulacrum,
ersatz revenant of residual need—

wouldn't that mean that nothing could halt the more
invisible than radiation flow
of you inside me, not the skull plates, not

the densest, least accessible twisted folds
of brain—all now no more resistant to you
who are less than air than air is to the body?

Imagine being known that way—the whole mind
boundlessly open to your vagrant hearing,
an audible palimpsest with every level—

from the sincerest argot of our old
concern, what I would have you hear, *I will
not fail to meet thee*, down to every moment's

muttering revery of feed me, fuck me,
the disused circuits of forgotten shame,
hard core of buried feeling—every level

echoing all at once and equally.
Better to think you'd shun me, if you could.
Better to think the silence when I call

is your refusal, and that you refuse
not in disgust but in devotion to
the partialities you knew me as.

The Table

Here is the phantom solace of a table,
shimmer of candlelight in every glass,
at every place an incandescent hovering
out of nowhere of somebody's face,

amnesia of the iron dark receding
bit by bit as feature after feature
shapes all around you brief fluorescences
of recognition, flickering on and off,

and for a moment you are niece again
in those eyes, friend in those, acquaintance, cousin,
granddaughter, great-granddaughter, on and on
the faces dimmer as they stretch away

into irrelevance along the table,
each one your emissary now, the closest,
the most remote, all burnishing the dark
to different shades of this familial dream,

this child's dream, mine, what I have left to give you:
Now you can sit among them, unafraid,
not minding even as the obsolete
distinctions they've put on to welcome you

begin dissolving, and you lift the glass
they lift, and drink the wine they drink, and see
your lips now anybody's lips reflected
in the wine you lower as they lower it.

The Summoning

There is the room. There is the fire in the grate,
sap fizzling out loose tentacles of steam
along the fluent borders of the burning,

its light diffusing as it grades away
to darkness an unwavering presumption
not of my somehow being here again,

but of my never having left. The way
each thing so certain of itself as mine
as I arranged it still assumes my seeing

with an ordinary absentmindedness,
the way the carpet's crushed pile signifies
the pressure of my heel, the dented pillow—

the posture and exact weight of a pleasure
that isn't pain subsiding but the body's
still undisproved belief that this is only

another evening after a long day,
a squandering on myself of instances
I have no end of. Even the calm implies

only the minor havoc of what might soon
disperse it: isn't there dinner to prepare?
couldn't the phone ring at any moment?

Where is my daughter? What is it I've forgotten?
Whose version of myself is this? Whose room
but yours, my dreaming brother? I see you now.

For you I bring my hand down through the fire.
It is for your sake that the flames rise through it.
What is it you are reaching out to hold,

to cling to, but your waking? Time to wake.
Time to embrace this, now your dreaming's over.
This is the nature now of all I am.

Scarecrow

Something got loose. The moment wasn't the moment
when the day cracked, and the crows poured through it,
splitting the air wide open in a gale
of black wings sweeping down across the yard,
into the trees, all jubilantly yelling,
yelling hysterically as they scattered away.

The moment wasn't the moment. Something got loose,
hunting the vision of itself, scenting
the trace of it across the words I wrote,
each word a veil and what the veil held back,
both caged and cage, until the letters loosened,
pulled from the page, and fluttered up around me

and all at once black night beyond the stars,
the outer space within the smallest atom,
flickered among the branches, over leaf sheen,
crazing the shimmery surfaces of air
and tree, and green yard where my feet were fixed,
my arms spread out, my two eyes opened wide.